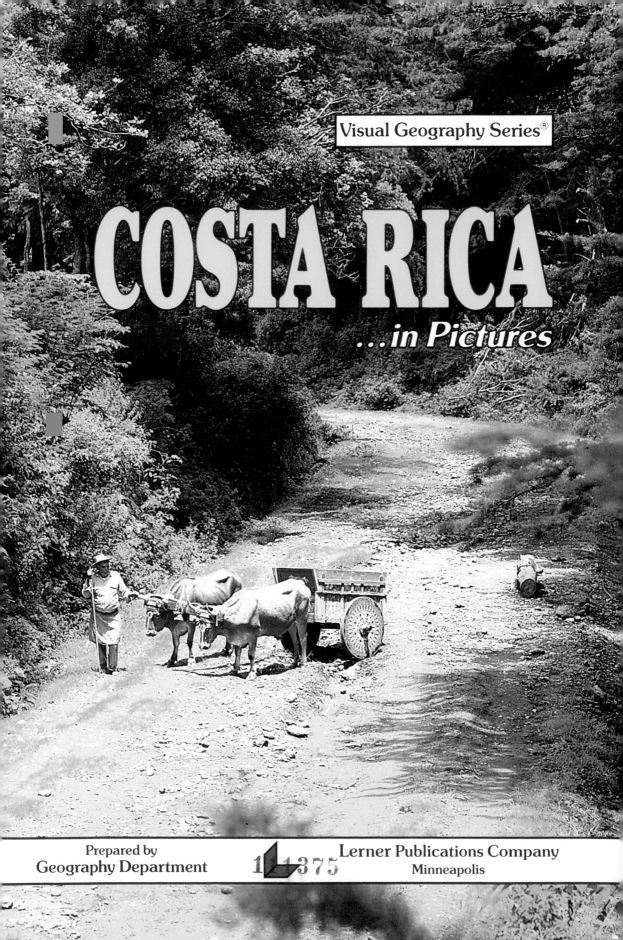

Visual Geography Series®

COSTA RICA
...in Pictures

Prepared by
Geography Department

Lerner Publications Company
Minneapolis

VISUAL GEOGRAPHY SERIES®

Publisher
Harry Jonas Lerner
Associate Publisher
Nancy M. Campbell
Executive Series Editor
Lawrence J. Zwier
Assistant Series Editor
Mary M. Rodgers
Editorial Assistant
Nora W. Kniskern
Illustrations Editor
Nathan A. Haverstock
Consultants/Contributors
Sandra K. Davis
Dr. Ruth F. Hale
Nathan A. Haverstock
Designer
Jim Simondet
Cartographer
Carol F. Barrett
Indexer
Kristine S. Schubert
Production Manager
Richard J. Hannah

Courtesy of Costa Rican Information Service

Some rivers in Costa Rica are rocky – a challenge for white-
water rafters and fishermen.

This is an all-new edition of the Visual Geography
Series. Previous editions have been published by
Sterling Publishing Company, New York City, and
some of the original textual information has been retained. New photographs, maps, charts, captions, and
updated information have been added. The text has
been entirely reset in 10/12 Century Textbook.

LIBRARY OF CONGRESS CATALOGING-IN-PUBLICATION DATA

Costa Rica in pictures.

(Visual geography series)
Rev. ed. of: Costa Rica in pictures / by Sandra Sawicki.
Includes index.
Summary: Photographs and brief text introduce the
geography, history, government, people, and economy
of Costa Rica.
1. Costa Rica. [1. Costa Rica] I. Sawicki, Sandra. Costa
Rica in pictures. II. Lerner Publications Company.
Geography Dept. III. Series: Visual geography series
(Minneapolis, Minn.)
F1543.C84   1987   972.86   86-20029
ISBN 0-8225-1805-8 (lib. bdg.)

International Standard Book Number: 0-8225-1805-8
Library of Congress Catalog Card Number: 86-20029

Courtesy of Inter-American Development Bank

Wooden components are cut to size at a furniture factory
in Jicaral.

Acknowledgments

Title page photo courtesy of Costa Rican Information Service.

Elevation contours adapted from *The Times Atlas of
the World*, seventh comprehensive edition (New York:
Times Books, 1985).

3 4 5 6 7 8 9 10 96 95 94 93 92 01 90 89

Courtesy of Inter-American Development Bank

A newly installed electricity meter at a Nicoya Peninsula home indicates the extent of Costa Rica's power grid. Although they are homesteading remote land, José Esteban Muñoz and his wife María enjoy the benefits of electric power.

Contents

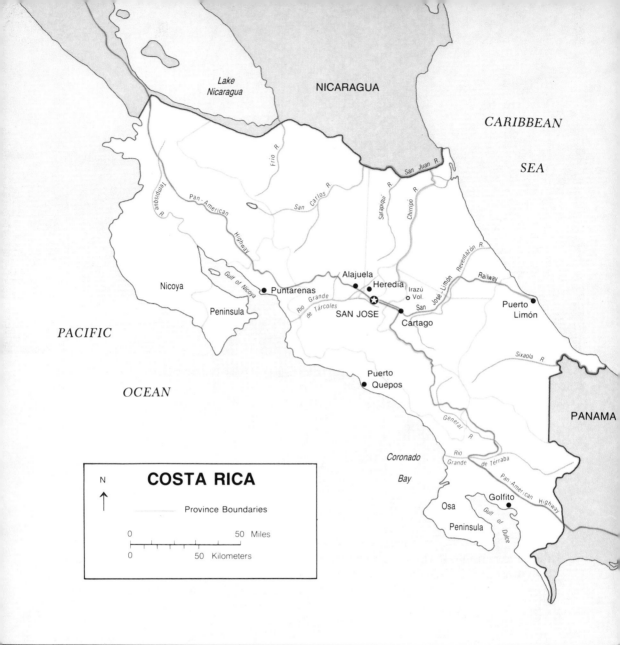

COSTA RICA

N

Province Boundaries

0   50 Miles

0   50 Kilometers

NICARAGUA

Lake Nicaragua

CARIBBEAN

SEA

Frío R.

San Juan R.

San Carlos R.

Sarapiquí R.

Chirripó R.

Pan-American Highway

Tempisque R.

Gulf of Nicoya

Nicoya Peninsula

PACIFIC

OCEAN

Puntarenas

Rio Grande de Tárcoles

Alajuela

Heredia

SAN JOSE

Cartago

Irazú Vol.

San Jose-Limón

Reventazón R.

Railway

Puerto Limón

Sixaola R.

Puerto Quepos

General R.

Coronado Bay

Rio Grande de Terraba

Pan-American Highway

PANAMA

Osa Peninsula

Golfito

Gulf of Dulce

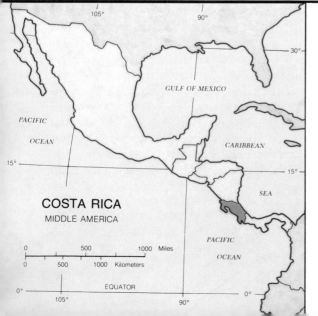

105°

90°

30°

GULF OF MEXICO

PACIFIC OCEAN

CARIBBEAN

15°

15°

SEA

COSTA RICA

MIDDLE AMERICA

PACIFIC OCEAN

0   500   1000 Miles

0   500   1000 Kilometers

0°

EQUATOR

0°

105°

90°

METRIC CONVERSION CHART
To Find Approximate Equivalents

WHEN YOU KNOW:	MULTIPLY BY:	TO FIND:
AREA		
acres	0.41	hectares
square miles	2.59	square kilometers
CAPACITY		
gallons	3.79	liters
LENGTH		
feet	30.48	centimeters
yards	0.91	meters
miles	1.61	kilometers
MASS (weight)		
pounds	0.45	kilograms
tons	0.91	metric tons
VOLUME		
cubic yards	0.77	cubic meters
TEMPERATURE		
degrees Fahrenheit	0.56 (*after* subtracting 32)	degrees Celsius

The area around the village of Santa María de Dota typifies the setting of many Central Plateau towns—a wide valley, surrounding farmlands, and mountains in the distance.

Introduction

Like a buoyant cork on troubled seas, Costa Rica is riding out the rough waters that have engulfed its Central American neighbors. The democratic republic is navigating the storm with self-reliance, a determination to remain as neutral as possible and still retain good relations with the United States, and a deep faith that its current troubles, like so many in its past, will pass.

Costa Rica is favored with a largely homogenous people and fertile farmlands. Unlike other Central American nations, Costa Rica has earned a reputation for political stability. It has in fact survived and flourished without a standing army for more than a third of a century. Through the twentieth century, political parties in Costa Rica have developed a tradition—broken only twice—of passing power to one another peacefully. Freely elected governments have enacted far-reaching educational and social programs—later copied by other governments similarly disposed to serving their people.

Throughout its history, Costa Rica's geographic isolation from more aggressive neighbors helped forge a vigorous spirit of quiet independence. Costa Rica was the last of the future Central American nations to be discovered and settled. Lacking gold and silver in any appreciable quantity, the colony of Costa Rica received little attention during three centuries of Spanish imperial rule. But step by step the hardy Spaniards who came to homestead its vast and beautiful central highlands created communities. Independence from Spain came easily, with little bloodshed, but immediately thereafter Costa Rica had

5

Courtesy of Costa Rican Information Service

The narrow-gauge railway linking San José and the Caribbean port of Limón affords travelers spectacular views of mountains, rushing rivers, and fertile valleys.

Latin America's most progressive countries. It was the first nation in Latin America to end slavery (in 1813) and to abolish punishment by death (in 1882). Over a century ago, Costa Rica began a system of free and compulsory education. In the late 1940s Costa Rica did away with its army and is now guarded by a small police force.

In 1987 Costa Rican president Oscar Arias Sánchez brought his nation into the limelight by sponsoring a regional peace plan. Signed in Guatemala and dubbed the Guatemala Accord, the document received the endorsement of the governmental heads of Nicaragua, El Salvador, Guatemala, and Honduras. Arias realized that Costa Rica's peace and prosperity were linked to the nonviolent resolution of regional conflicts. He, therefore, made a strong attempt to ease Central America's tensions with Central American ideas. Although only Costa Rica has completely complied with the accord, some progress has been made in addressing local issues by the other countries that agreed to the plan.

to resist encroachment by some of its more powerful neighbors.

By the mid-nineteenth century, the young nation began to emerge as one of

This pre-Columbian work of art decorates the lawn of the Cariari Hotel and Country Club near San José. The hotel, which shows English-language movies via closed-circuit television in all the rooms, caters to visitors from the United States.

Courtesy of Costa Rican Information Service

A construction boom in San José has brought office towers and high-rise apartment buildings to the cityscape. Yet, with its many single-story buildings and broad, tree-lined streets, the city retains a provincial air.

1) The Land

The Republic of Costa Rica, the third smallest Central American nation (after Belize and El Salvador), has a total land area of 19,600 square miles, making it roughly the size of Vermont and New Hampshire combined, or about two-thirds the size of Scotland. Costa Rica measures 288 miles at its greatest length, from northwest to southeast, and 170 miles at its widest point, in the north. The width narrows to only 74 miles in the southern portion of the nation.

..._ .38-mile-long northern boundary with Nicaragua is formed partly by the San Juan River system, which flows into the Caribbean. On the south, Costa Rica's border with Panama is 190 miles in length. Portions of this border area were long in dispute, and the present boundary was not formally ;   ' to by both nations until 1941.

Costa Rica's eastern and western limits are formed by the Caribbean Sea and the Pacific Ocean. The Caribbean coast is

Much of central Costa Rica consists of rolling land that provides accessible pasture for the nation's cattle herds.

relatively level and open, in marked contrast to the nation's jagged and physically diverse profile on the Pacific side. Two peninsulas shaped like hooks jut out from the Pacific coastline—the Guanacaste (or Nicoya) Peninsula to the north, and the smaller Osa Peninsula in the south. Deep gulfs and bays punctuate the balance of the country's western shores. Major bays include the Gulf of Nicoya, tucked between Guanacaste Peninsula and the coast; Coronado Bay, which hugs the central and south central shore; and the Gulf of Dulce between the Osa Peninsula and the mainland.

There are numerous islands off Costa Rica's Pacific coast. The best known is Cocos Island, located 300 miles offshore. Deserted and covered with woods and rocks, tiny Cocos has strategic value because of its proximity to the Panama Canal. It is also widely known as the site of possible buried pirate treasure—specula-

tion arising from the island's history as a refuge for sea-raiders.

Topography

Costa Rica lacks the spectacular scenery of many Latin American countries. Much of the land consists of gently rolling hills, with here and there an occasional volcano to add a dramatic accent.

The nation's three principal natural regions are determined by altitude. First, there are low plains and tropical rainforests along both coasts at elevations of less than 3,200 feet. Second, the fertile and healthful Central Plateau is situated at altitudes ranging from 3,200 feet to 6,500 feet. Finally, cool mountain highlands rise to altitudes above 6,500 feet. Four mountain chains run from northwest to southeast, with some peaks exceeding 12,500 feet—the Guanacaste, Tilarán, Central, and Talamanca ranges.

Along the Pacific, both mountains and grassy plains are to be found. The Guanacaste Mountains, the westernmost range, run parallel to the wide coastal lowlands and end in the north in low foothills some 70 miles from the western end of the frontier with Nicaragua. Interrupted only occasionally by coastal hills, plains of sand and clay fringe Costa Rica's Pacific shores from the Osa Peninsula northward to the port of Puntarenas.

Farther north, the Pacific coastal plains broaden until finally they merge with the Guanacaste Plain near the Gulf of Nicoya. These lowlands are shielded from heavy tropical rainfall by the eastern slopes of the Guanacaste Mountains. This natural shelter results in droughts on the plains, even though the rainy season there extends from May to December each year.

Volcanic ash deposited over many centuries by erupting volcanoes has enriched the soils of the Pacific coast, making them fertile for farming. The harsh dry climate of this region—inhabited by relatively few subsistence farmers and cattlemen—has held back the growth of population.

In contrast, thick vegetation covers the eastern lowlands, which extend down from Nicaragua in the north and run along Costa Rica's entire Caribbean coast. These Caribbean lowlands are broad in the north, become narrow near Puerto Limón, and once again spread out as they meet the delta of the Sixaola River in the south. The soils of the Caribbean coast are also volcanic in origin, though Costa Rica's prevailing winds now blow from the northeast to the southwest, with the result that Caribbean coast soils are not being renewed with wind-blown volcanic ash.

Along with its lush vegetation, the Caribbean region of Costa Rica has a hot, humid climate. Settlement in the Carib-

The sand on many of the beaches along the Caribbean coast, like this one on Tortuguero Island, is black. Wave action over the course of many centuries has reduced chunks of dark, glassy volcanic rock to mere grains of sand.

Courtesy of Costa Rican Information Service

9

bean lowlands did not occur until the late nineteenth century, when bananas were introduced. Heavy rainfall, good soils, and infrequent windstorms have promoted the cultivation of bananas in this region ever since.

Meseta Central (Central Plateau)

The most important geographical area of Costa Rica is the Meseta Central, or Central Plateau—an area that supports three-fourths of the nation's population and almost all of its industry and farming. The Central Plateau has an area of 3,500 square miles and is situated at altitudes ranging from 3,200 to 6,500 feet, between the Central and Talamanca mountains. Rural population density in the region is among the highest in Latin America.

The Central Plateau is contoured by rolling hills and, on the northern rim, by a series of volcanoes. Rich soils combine with an invigorating springlike climate and frost-free temperatures to make the Central Plateau ideal for most kinds of farming. Practically all of Costa Rica's coffee production is concentrated here, as is the raising of livestock and the cultivation of such crops as maize, rice, sugar, and vegetables.

The Central Plateau itself is divided into two basins by a low range of volcanic hills that form the Continental Divide. To the east lies the Cartago Basin, with an elevation of 5,000 feet. This basin is generally wetter and warmer than its western counterpart, the San José Basin, whose elevation is from 3,000 to 4,000 feet.

Another upland basin, the General Valley, is situated to the south of the Meseta

Courtesy of Inter-American Development Bank

Costa Rica's forests yield many useful woods, such as these large cedar logs being mounted in a lathe. As each log turns, the lathe cuts wood from it in thin sheets that will then be used to make plywood.

A tranquil scene at the water-filled crater of the Irazú Volcano.

Central and the Talamanca Mountains. Similar in size to the Central Plateau, the General Valley forms a depression of plains, terraces, and hills at elevations of only 1,000 to 3,500 feet above the sea. It arcs southward to coastal mountains in southwestern Costa Rica. Settlement in the General Valley has taken place only in the last several decades, as farmers have migrated there to escape overcrowded conditions on the Central Plateau.

The last of Costa Rica's major topographical areas is found amidst the country's mountain and volcanic ranges. At altitudes over 6,500 feet, the terrain is rough and the climate cold. Too harsh to support farming, some of the cold mountain uplands have been converted into pastures.

Mountains and Volcanoes

Scattered throughout the nation's mountain ranges there are peaks of substantial

Grande is the highest at 12,532 feet, followed by Mount Terbi at 12,513 feet and Mount Kámuk at 11,688 feet.

The volcanoes of Costa Rica are sources of both beauty and destruction. Frequent eruptions have caused thousands of deaths and brought economic ruin. At the same time, the conical symmetry of volcanic peaks adds distinction and dimension to the landscape.

Mount Irazú, near Cartago, is the best known of the volcanoes. It made gruesome headlines in 1963, 1965, and 1967, when it sent tons of ash down into the San José Basin and left most of the region's dairy and cattle lands buried. Despite the potential danger of another eruption from Irazú—which rises in height to 11,417 feet—tourists are allowed the memorable thrill of peering down into its crater.

In August 1968, Mount Arenal, another volcano in the Guanacaste Range, erupted and poured hot ash over nearby cattle

11

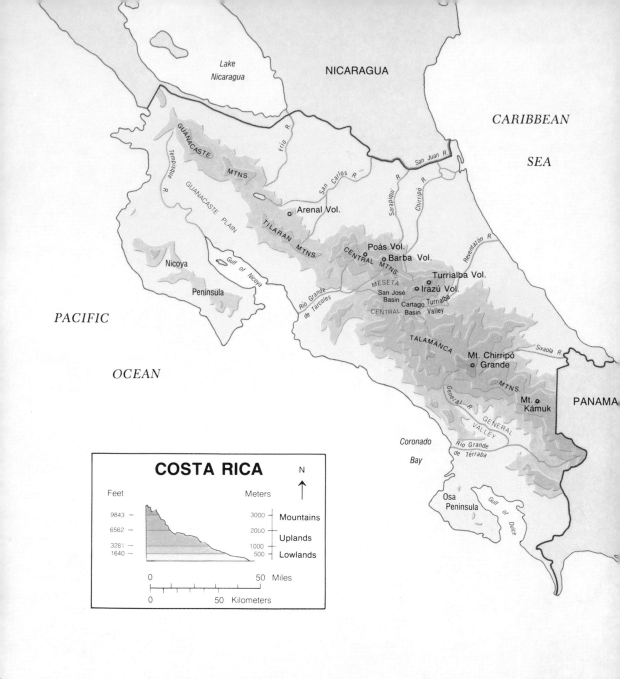

COSTA RICA

Feet		Meters	
9843 —		3000 —	Mountains
6562 —		2000 —	Uplands
3281 —		1000 —	
1640 —		500 —	Lowlands

0   50   Miles

0   50   Kilometers

lands. Thousands of animals were killed outright, and some 80,000 others, without pastures on which to feed, had to be slaughtered for immediate sale.

Other famous Costa Rican volcanoes are Poás (9,055 feet), Barba (9,612 feet), and Turrialba (11,220 feet)—all located on the Central Plateau north of San José.

Waterways

Costa Rica's rivers are not suited for navigation except in the lowlands. In northern and northeastern parts of the nation, the major river system is the San Juan, which rises in Lake Nicaragua—a vast lake just across the Nicaraguan border. Four tributaries of the San Juan network rise in

Costa Rica—the Frío, San Carlos, Sarapiquí, and Chirripó.

To the west, the Tempisque River and its branches rise in the Guanacaste Plain and empty into the Gulf of Nicoya. In the central area, two rivers provide drainage—the Reventazón, which rises near Cartago and eventually enters the Caribbean, and the Río Grande de Tárcoles, which rises north of the Reventazón on the Central Plateau and flows into the Pacific near Puntarenas. In the southeast, the major network consists of the Sixaola River and its tributaries, and in the southwest, the General River and the Río Grande de Térraba provide drainage.

Since Costa Rica has both lowlands and high plateaus, temperatures and rainfall vary according to altitude. On the west coast where the land slopes from an altitude of 1,500 feet down to the sea, daytime temperatures range from 85° to 90° F. Rainfall is moderate to heavy—about 40 inches annually in the northwest and 80 to 120 inches in the south. The Caribbean coast, with land rising from the sea to 2,000 feet, swelters at 80° to 100° F during the day. Up to 80 inches of rain pound the area yearly, producing a steamy and swampy environment.

The Central Plateau's weather is agreeable all year round, with temperatures of 75° to 80° F in the daytime and 60° F in the evenings. Precipitation in San José averages almost 74 inches annually—most of it, however, occurs between May and November. In the relatively dry winters, rainfall amounts to less than 10 inches for

The low coastal plain near Tortuguero National Park is hot, humid, and heavily forested. Because of the inhospitable climate, this region is one of the least populated parts of Costa Rica.

The Río Grande de Tárcoles is one of several rivers dammed to provide water power for the La Garita power plant.

A quiet path winds through a forest area near Santa Cruz, on the Nicoya Peninsula.

Flora

Forests and woods cover almost 60 percent of Costa Rica's territory. The more familiar and commercially prized species are laurel, Spanish cedar, juniper, oak, mahogany, balsa, and ebony, while on the high mountain slopes are stands of pine trees.

In the wet Caribbean lowlands, palms and tree ferns are abundant, along with a great variety of orchids and bromeliads (plants of the pineapple family). Liana, a climbing plant with woody vines, often grows to great size in the tropical rain-forests. A common tree is the ceiba, or silk-cotton tree, which yields a silky fiber called kapok. The Pacific lowlands are characterized by savannas—grasslands with scattered trees—where ceibas and numerous other trees rise from beds of grasses, sedges, and flowering plants of many types.

Much valuable forest land in northeastern Costa Rica near the Nicaraguan border remains undisturbed because transportation facilities are inadequate. In other areas, with the opening of roads, timberland has usually been destroyed. Marginal farmers, who burn parts of the forest in order to develop their croplands, have not only destroyed some Costa Rican forest resources but also depleted valuable soil nutrients, which are not replaced by nature for a long time.

Fauna

Costa Rica possesses a wealth of animals, including varieties found in both South and North America. In the dense rain-forests, typical animal life includes a variety of tree-dwelling monkeys and opossums, as well as toads, frogs, and such reptiles as iguanas and snakes. Birds—macaws, parrots, parakeets—and insects (some of them disease carriers) are very prolific in

Costa Rica's wet lowlands. Large cats such as jaguars and pumas roam the tropical forests and plains, and in the same region one can find examples of North American white-tailed deer, small rodents, flesh-eating birds (owls, hawks, and vultures), as well as harmless quail and partridge.

Mineral Resources

Compared to some other Latin American nations, Costa Rica has little mineral wealth, and mining has never been of much economic importance. Most ores that exist are of low grade, though Puntarenas Province has some small gold deposits and manganese has been found farther north in Guanacaste. Other minerals found only in small quantities include iron ore on the Nicoya Peninsula and sulfur near San Carlos. Salt production from the sea ᴇ ᴀt 10,000 tons annually.

Pelicans ride at anchor in the Gulf of Nicoya near the rich fishing beds off Puntarenas. Costa Rica's jagged Pacific coastline is indented by many scenic inlets that provide calm anchorage for fishing boats.

... is native to Costa Rica. The bushes on which the flower grows can approach the size of a small tree.

Cities

SAN JOSE

Since 1823, the capital city of San José has dominated the political, cultural, and economic activity of the nation. It serves as the nation's primary commercial center and provides a market for local farm goods. Several railroads link San José with ports on the Caribbean Sea and the Pacific Ocean.

Perched on the Central Plateau at an ideal elevation of 3,870 feet, San José is a city of tree-shaded and orderly streets. It also has numerous parks, where Sunday afternoon concerts and relaxing promenades are a ritual for the *Josefinos* (those who live in San José). Architectural styles follow European or North American models, rather than the classic Iberian (Spanish, Portuguese, or Basque) styles typical of other Central American nations.

The population of San José is about 273,000, and an estimated 307,000 more live in the surrounding area. San José was founded in 1751 by Spanish traders and settlers. Although one of the last of Costa Rica's cities to be established, San José quickly prospered and grew. Over 60 percent of people living in the nation's urban areas live in San José, and its growth rate continues to far exceed that of the total population.

HEREDIA

Three other cities of importance share the Central Plateau with San José. Heredia (population 30,000) is only six miles to the northwest of San José and is situated in the shadow of the Poás Volcano. It has a Spanish colonial atmosphere that derives from its Andalusian heritage. Heredia's economy is based upon agriculture—especially coffee and cattle—and industry.

ALAJUELA

Eight miles due west of Heredia is Alajuela, the gateway to Ojo de Agua, a

An Iberian-inspired grille covers a window in Heredia, a city originally settled by Andalusians.

much-visited swimming resort fed by a powerful mountain spring. With a population of 43,000, Alajuela not only shares the loveliness of Central Plateau cities but also is a key city in the Costa Rican economy. It is the site of Costa Rica's largest granary and a major center for sugar growers, cattle raisers, and lumber and coffee producers.

CARTAGO

The nation's first capital city, Cartago, is situated in a coffee-growing area, 14 miles to the southeast of San José. Founded in 1564 by Juan Vásquez de Coronado—Costa Rica's first governor—Cartago has architecture and traditions rooted in colonial history. Because of its location at the foot of Mount Irazú, this city of 28,000 was leveled by earthquakes and volcanic activity in 1841 and 1910 but, with extensive rebuilding, has risen up anew from destruction like the legendary phoenix.

PORTS

Puerto Limón (or simply Limón) witnessed the arrival of sixteenth-century Spanish explorers. Today Limón, with approximately 42,000 inhabitants, is the nation's busiest Caribbean port. Limón was originally called Cariari by the Indians who lived there when the galleon carrying Christopher Columbus anchored offshore in 1502.

Limón is now the hub of the banana region along the Caribbean and the chief point of exit for Costa Rica's exports to its trading partners throughout the world. Despite Limón's importance to the nation's economy, a road linking this city with San José was opened only a few years ago. Before then it was necessary for one to fly between Limón and San José—or ride the railway over a scenic though tiring route.

Three other Costa Rican ports are located in Puntarenas Province on the Pacific. Puntarenas itself (35,000 people) is the fourth largest city in Costa Rica, and from its docks, shipments of canned fish, sugar, coconuts, and cattle move overseas. At the tip of Coronado Bay, Puerto Quepos, once important for its banana trade, acts now as a focal point for coastal shipping among Costa Rica's Pacific ports. Golfito, near the Panamanian frontier, is the chief banana port of the nation. It was originally developed by the United Fruit Company, which introduced banana plantations to the Pacific after the fruit was grown successfully on the Caribbean coast.

Courtesy of Costa Rican Information Service

Despite a great deal of urban growth, San José has retained its pleasant aspect, with plenty of greenery and open space devoted to parks.

This ornate tablelike sculpture is called a *metate* and was used by the Huetar Indians as an altar and as a stone on which to grind corn. The Huetars inhabited the Central Plateau and the Pacific lowlands before the coming of the Spaniards.

2) History and Government

Before its discovery by Europeans, Costa Rica was inhabited by an estimated 27,000 Indians of diverse tribal origin. The principal Indian tribes—namely, the Chorotegas, Caribs, Borucas, Corobicis, and Nahuas—were engaged primarily in hunting and farming. Their cultures were generally less advanced than many of the pre-Columbian civilizations to the north and south.

On his fourth and last voyage to the Americas, Christopher Columbus set out in 1502 to explore the Central American coastline from Honduras to Panama. During a violent late-summer storm, he and his crew sought safety in Cariari Bay near present-day Puerto Limón. A party of men led by Columbus's brother, Bartolomé, scouted the surrounding area and made contact with bands of Indians—whose magnificent golden jewelry and ornamental costumes dazzled the explorers.

On the strength of this encounter, Columbus and his men assumed they had accidentally discovered an area of vast mineral wealth and thus named the region Costa Rica, which means "rich coast" in Spanish. Fortune hunters who followed Columbus's men learned to their dismay that no such riches existed. Instead they found an unhealthy climate along the coast and hostile Indians who refused to submit to Spanish control.

Colonization

The Spaniards, led by Francisco Fernández de Córdoba, founded their first settlement in Costa Rica 22 years after Columbus's landing. Essentially an outpost near what is today Puntarenas, it was named Bruselas.

In 1561, Juan de Cavallón—with a band of 90 Spaniards and some Negro slaves—established the city of Garcimuñoz on the Nicoya Peninsula, and from there Cavallón led expeditions into the Costa Rican interior. Failing to find gold, Cavallón left and was succeeded by Juan Vásquez de Coronado.

Vásquez de Coronado was friendly toward the Indians and thus succeeded—where his predecessors had failed—in establishing control over them. He also opened the door to Spanish homesteaders and introduced cattle, horses, and swine to the region. Coronado's wise administration came to an abrupt end when, returning to Spain to seek funds for the colony, he was lost at sea.

In 1573, King Philip II of Spain formally defined the permanent boundaries of Costa Rica and placed the country under the jurisdiction of the colonial government of the captaincy general in Guatemala.

Until the late eighteenth century, Costa Rica remained the least developed and poorest country on the Central American isthmus. Ferocious bands of Miskito Indians swept down into Costa Rica from Nicaragua and continually harassed the colonists by pillaging farms and plantations and, in one instance, murdering the governor of Costa Rica. Settlements along both the Caribbean and Pacific coasts were constantly raided by French, Dutch, and English pirates, who forced the closing of ports and stifled what little trade Costa Rica had with the outside world.

Trade policies dictated by the mother country—including a prohibition on commerce between the Spanish colonies and all

Independent Picture Service

Golden trinkets of various sizes—worn by pre-Columbian Indians—inspired the conquistadors to give Costa Rica its name, which means "rich coast."

other countries except Spain—slowed down progress in Costa Rica. The small colonial population, numbering less than 20,000, lived in fear of marauders and in almost total isolation from the rest of Central America. Lacking transportation, education, medical facilities, and even adequate clothing, the colonists—who for the most part had emigrated from the Spanish regions of Galicia, Estremadura, Aragón, and Andalusia—had to work hard to scrape a primitive existence from the land.

At the close of the eighteenth century, Spain elevated all but one of its Central American provinces to the rank of *intendencia*—a status that allowed local governors to exercise greater control over financial and judicial affairs. The exception was Costa Rica, which was placed under the control of Nicaragua and given a lower status in the administrative structure.

The Nineteenth Century

On September 15, 1821, Guatemala declared its independence from Spain. When news of the break reached Costa Rica one month later, the colonists voted to do the same. Shortly thereafter, while in the process of creating its own form of self-government, Costa Rica received word from General Agustín de Iturbide, self-proclaimed emperor of Mexico, urging immediate annexation to his empire. The citizens of Heredia and Cartago supported annexation to Mexico, while the residents of San José and Alajuela looked upon Iturbide's demand as nothing short of imperialism and chose independence.

The conflict brought about a short civil war, which was won in 1823 by the *independistas*, who then moved the capital city from Cartago to San José. In the same year, Iturbide's government fell and Costa Rica joined the newly created Federation of Central America. The first constitution of Costa Rica was written on January 22, 1825.

Photo by Dr. Roma Hoff

Buildings from Costa Rica's colonial past are found in many parts of the country. This Roman Catholic church was built in 1797—about 25 years before Costa Rica achieved independence from Spain—and stands in Heredia, near San José.

Independent Picture Service

These are the two sides of a coin struck by Costa Rica when it was still a member of the Federation of Central America.

The delicate *guaria morada*, a native orchid, is Costa Rica's national flower.

Perfect stone spheres have been found in no Latin American country except Costa Rica. Why, how, and by whom they were made remain mysteries.

The system of government set up by the Central American federation included a bicameral (two-house) legislature, a federation chief executive with jurisdiction over matters affecting the entire union, and local presidents—elected by each member nation—who exercised authority over local affairs.

JUAN MORA FERNANDEZ

Juan Mora Fernández was elected Costa Rica's first president under the federalized arrangement. Serving from 1824 to 1833, Mora Fernández headed a progressive administration. He encouraged education, undertook social reforms, and developed commerce. He initiated the practice of giving away free land to anyone who agreed to raise coffee, and coffee soon became Costa Rica's chief export.

Mora Fernández also managed to keep Costa Rica free of the civil strife that continually disrupted the other Central American states. The intense political discord among the other members of the federation was not supported by Costa

Independent Picture Service

Juan Mora Fernández, commemorated by this statue, served as Costa Rica's first president after the country joined the Federation of Central America in 1823.

Courtesy of Museum of Modern Art of Latin America

The Brunca Indians, who lived long ago in southwestern Costa Rica near Panama, made these ceramic figures of a man and of a woman (on the right) carrying a baby. The style shows the influence of more advanced cultures in South America.

Ricans. Manifesting its traditionally independent national character, Costa Rica decided to withdraw from the federation in 1838.

BRAULIO CARRILLO COLINA

Costa Rica is generally credited with a history of democratic and fair-minded presidents. This is not to say that the nation has had no *caudillos,* or strong-man politicians. Braúlio Carrillo Colina, who governed from 1835 to 1837 and then again from 1838 to 1842, easily falls into this category. Carrillo first came to the presidential office through a congressional election when his predecessor, José Rafael de Gallegos, resigned.

As president, Carrillo encouraged the development of legal codes, organized the juridical system, constructed roads and schools, and reformed the landholding system. Despite this enlightenment, he suppressed any and all opposition, especially that voiced by people from cities other than San José.

Independent Picture Service

General Francisco Morazán, a Honduran, was the last president of the ill-fated Federation of Central America (which included Costa Rica). He later ousted Braúlio Carrillo Colina from the Costa Rican presidency but was himself forced from office and executed in 1842.

Francisco Morazán, a Honduran and former chief executive of the then-dissolved Central American federation, eventually succeeded Carrillo. When he tried to restore the broken Central American union by force, however, a revolt forced him to abandon the presidency and he was subsequently taken prisoner and executed.

CONSTITUTION OF 1848

Despite somewhat unstable governments that followed, a new constitution was drawn up in 1848 that officially declared Costa Rica an independent republic. The most significant feature of the document was the abolition of the army as a permanent institution and the substitution of a civilian guard. The absence of a standing army continues to distinguish Costa Rica today from most other nations of the world.

From 1824 to 1889, Costa Rica had 25 presidents. Seven used force to gain office, eleven were chosen in noncompetitive elections, and six were legally named for brief periods. Only one chief executive came to office in a competitive election.

The relative stability of Costa Rica, however, helped attract numerous emigrants from Europe. In the mid-1800s many Spaniards came to the peaceful nation, as did other Europeans and refugees from other Central American countries. In 1844, the total national population was 80,000, and by 1860 that figure had risen to 125,000.

WILLIAM WALKER

Costa Rica was aroused to take up arms against Nicaragua in 1856, when William Walker, a notorious soldier of fortune from the United States, gained control of Nicaragua's government and threatened to do the same in Costa Rica. President Juan Rafael Mora Porras ordered Costa Rican troops into Nicaragua to help expel Walker from Central America. The combined forces of Nicaragua, Guatemala, El Salvador, and Costa Rica succeeded in

Independent Picture Service

William Walker, a military adventurer from the United States, proclaimed himself ruler of Nicaragua in 1856 and launched a campaign to conquer all of Central America. His invasion of Costa Rica was thwarted when his command post in Guanacaste province was surrounded and burned.

parties that had been built around them. He also abolished congress and replaced the constitution with a new one that lasted for 75 years.

Guardia silenced all political comment, put his friends and relatives into key positions, and nearly exhausted the national treasury. It seems none of Costa Rica's dictatorial leaders were total villains, however. This was true of Guardia also, for he advanced public education, ended capital punishment, provided liberal incentives to coffee and sugar producers, and enjoyed favorable press abroad until his death in 1882.

Guardia's finest legacy was the construction of a railway from San José to the Caribbean coast. He asked Minor Keith, a U.S. citizen whose uncle had built railways in Peru and Chile, to undertake its construction. By 1890 the project was completed at a cost of $8 million and 4,000

forcing Walker to relinquish power in May 1857. President Mora emerged from this skirmish a national hero.

Immediately after the close of that war—which left 10,000 Costa Ricans dead —a dispute broke out between Nicaragua and Costa Rica over rights to the San Juan River along their border. With the threat of war once again shrouding the isthmus, El Salvador stepped in to mediate, and a treaty was signed preventing an armed conflict.

DICTATORSHIP OF GUARDIA

For many years after independence, an oligarchy of a few prominent families with large agricultural interests dominated Costa Rican politics. Then, in 1870, General Tomás Guardia Gutiérrez seized power and established a military dictatorship. Guardia sent members of the former elite into exile and dissolved the political

Independent Picture Service

This monument to Juan Santamaría in Alajuela memorializes a young soldier who died in the war of 1856 against Nicaragua. He is considered a national hero.

Courtesy of Museum of Modern Art of Latin America

President Juan Rafael Mora Porras, a national hero who is commemorated in this statue, led Costa Rica's forces to victory over William Walker.

lives. Tropical diseases killed most of the railway construction crew, and the builders were eventually forced to hire Jamaicans to finish the job.

To create freight traffic for the new line, Keith also introduced banana plantations along the railway route. He thus established one of Costa Rica's most profitable industries. By the end of the nineteenth century, Keith's plantations and those of his competitors were merged into the United Fruit Company—now United Brands.

Development of Democracy

In the presidential elections of 1889, Costa Rica tried to achieve full-fledged representative democracy. For the first time, there were honest electoral procedures, open political debates by all candidates, and complete freedom of the press and speech. Prior to this election, voting had been noncompetitive and indirect. Prominent Costa Ricans had voted for local electors, who then selected regional electors, who finally elected the president and congress. Up until 1889, there had been little political activism among the citizens, who were not allowed to participate in the voting process.

Although not every election since 1889 has been completely fair—and corruption has not been completely absent from political parties—Costa Rica's record is better than those of most Latin American countries. For the most part, politics in Costa Rica has been marked by stability, respect for laws, aversion to unlimited presidential power, honest public administrations, and free expression.

Of the presidents in office after 1889, on-

ly two came to office by using force. Eight were chosen in noncompetitive elections, three were interim appointments, and most were chosen in free, contested elections. Another indication of Costa Rica's political maturity is that during 150 years of independence, the military has occupied the presidency for only 16 years—in marked contrast with the histories of most other Latin American nations.

Led by a torch bearer, high school students celebrate Independence Day (September 15) with a parade. Before regional conflict heated up in the late 1970s, a torch such as this was carried in a relay race from Guatemala to Panama—a way of commemorating that all the Central American countries gained independence simultaneously in 1821.

A public health worker administers oral polio vaccine to a young girl.

The Early Twentieth Century

Two political figures who stand out in the twentieth century are Cleto González Víquez and Ricardo Jiménez Oreamuno. Political foes, they nonetheless shared a desire to initiate social reforms. González Víquez, president from 1906 to 1910 and again from 1928 to 1932, ushered in a period of educational and democratic changes. He was succeeded by Jiménez Oreamuno, who served from 1910 to 1914, from 1924 to 1928, and from 1932 to 1936. Jiménez Oreamuno worked toward cultural and democratic development. He created a national insurance system, had the first minimum wage law passed, and distributed land purchased from the United Fruit Company to poor farmers.

Despite this progressive leadership and the economic expansion that was achieved even during a period of worldwide depression, most Costa Ricans did not share in the material gains of their country. Indeed, most people continued to live in poverty, without land, and with very little attention from the national government. In contrast, the interests of large landholders and the upper classes were well served by the government. Nonetheless, educational reforms had created a school system that awakened people to a desire for further political change and economic equality. In response to these stirrings, several new political parties took root, among them the Communist Party (later to be called the Popular Vanguard) in 1929.

Modern Era

The winner of the 1940 elections, Rafael Angel Calderón Guardia of the National Republican Party (PRN), instituted a popular regime that stressed social legislation. This emphasis on reform promptly alienated Calderón from wealthy, conservative elements, and he turned for support to the Popular Vanguard and other radical groups to the left. These were not strong enough, however, to enable Calderón to enforce the kind of social policy he advocated (including unemployment compensation, paid vacations, and social security). Amid rising tensions, Calderón's administration was accused by wavering supporters and middle-class intellectuals of being inept, corrupt, and fraudulent.

Calderón's protégé and PRN colleague, Teodoro Picado Michalski, won a narrow victory in the 1944 presidential elections. He was supported in his Calderón-inspired plans by an unlikely mixture of extreme right-wing and extreme left-wing elements. Strong opposition from these two opposing camps developed during Picado's term of office. The conservative National Union Party (PUN) under the leadership of Otilio Ulate Blanco, a leading newspaper publisher, opposed Picado's social projects and Communist sympathies. On the other side was the Social Democratic Party (PSD) led by José Figueres Ferrer, a prominent landowner. The PSD was composed of students, intellectuals, and middle-class businesspersons.

THE 1948 ELECTIONS

Heading into the 1948 elections, this opposition remained intact and faced Calderón, who was himself eligible for reelection as a PRN standard-bearer. After an intense and hard-fought campaign, Ulate Blanco emerged the winner by only 10,000 votes. But Calderón had powerful allies—the incumbent Picado administration, which refused to recognize the victory and claimed that an electoral technicality voided Ulate Blanco's election.

The turbulent events that followed this election and lasted for two months repre-sent Costa Rica's most serious political upheaval. Figueres massed arms and men at his coffee plantation and launched a revolt against the Calderón–Picado forces in Ulate Blanco's name. The rebels—with material assistance from Cuba, Guatemala, Honduras, and Nicaragua—quickly gained control of Limón and Cartago and soon surrounded San José. Calderón, Picado, and other PRN leaders fled the country. An interim junta with Figueres at its head was installed for 18 months to guarantee a smooth transition into the duly elected government of Ulate Blanco.

JOSE FIGUERES FERRER

José Figueres Ferrer, who managed this feat of acting as liaison, deserves a prominent place in Costa Rican history. Born in 1906, Figueres was educated as an engineer in Costa Rica and the United States. Like many other Latin men, he combined several careers—as a writer, political philosopher, coffee baron, and industrialist. In his native country and abroad, the name of this small and energetic leader came to stand for liberal democracy.

In the 1940s, Figueres organized the Social Democratic Party, which attracted progressive political thinkers who opposed President Calderón. Figueres himself achieved national fame in 1942 when he strongly denounced Calderón's ad-

The old style of public building is exemplified by the ornate Post Office Department building in San José, seen here as it appeared in the 1930s.

Independent Picture Service

ministration over the national radio. For this rash action, Figueres was exiled to Mexico for two years.

As president of the Founding Junta of the Second Republic of Costa Rica, which exercised almost dictatorial authority from 1948 to 1949, Figueres attempted to carry out reforms in the full knowledge that Calderón's defeated supporters might return to use force to upset his control. Because of his interest in farming, he encouraged the introduction of advanced technology to boost agricultural production. He enacted wide-ranging fiscal reforms and nationalized all banks. He disbanded the civilian guard and replaced it with a national police force of 1,000 and a coast guard of 700 men. Lastly, he provided for women's suffrage.

At Figueres's initiative, a constituent assembly was called to formulate a new constitution. In all, the Figueres-led junta helped calm down the local situation and pave the way for Ulate Blanco's inauguration, which took place without incident in November 1949.

Ulate Blanco respected Figueres's reforms and displayed moderation and wisdom in his measures to help restore stability. He averted a financial crisis by increasing trade with the United States and by strongly promoting Costa Rican exports.

While Ulate Blanco still held the presidential reins, Figueres and his followers banded together into a new political alliance, the National Liberation Party (PLN), which advocated swift economic and social reform. Figueres became the PLN candidate in the 1953 presidential elections and

This monument at Santa María de Dota honors the dead of Costa Rica's 1948 struggle to prevent a Communist takeover.

Volunteers wearing the colors of the National Liberation Party work for candidate Luis Alberto Monge in the 1980 presidential election.

Courtesy of Leanne Hogie

won by an overwhelming 65 percent of the vote. Figueres's popularity carried PLN congressional candidates along with him into the Legislative Assembly, where they controlled 65 percent of the seats.

As president, Figueres's success as a negotiator enabled him to work out a new deal with the United Fruit Company, historically the largest foreign economic interest in the country. Costa Rica was given

Young supporters of the Unity Party lend a hand during the 1980 presidential election. Political involvement by Costa Rica's citizens has helped shape the country's strong democratic tradition.

Courtesy of Leanne Hogie

31

a 35-percent share of all company profits—as against its earlier 10-percent share. The U.S.-owned firm also turned over its schools, hospitals, housing, and recreational facilities to control by the Costa Rican government. To Figueres's credit, relations between Costa Rica and the giant corporation remained cordial.

Figueres later created federal agencies to deal with urban development and housing. Among his other accomplishments were the further expansion of the public school system; the raising of minimum wages and income taxes; the nationalization of some banking facilities; and the introduction to the rural areas of medical clinics, electricity, running water, and sewage removal.

Though these achievements were applauded by Figueres's supporters, his critics voiced serious opposition to the lavish spending required to finance them. Figueres may have felt confident in spending at a time when coffee and banana prices were high, but opponents, fearful of inflation and economic collapse, urged more frugal policies for a nation tied to a strictly agriculture-based economy.

After Figueres left office in 1958, the presidency rotated between the PUN and the PLN. Figueres became the "grand old man" of the most influential political group of the country and remained active on the national scene. In 1970, he was again nominated for the presidency by his party and was elected to serve another term as chief executive until 1974.

The PLN continued to control the government in the mid-1980s, claiming over half of the seats in the Legislative Assembly. Economic problems—including large debts in the public sector, rising inflation and unemployment, and increasing rural poverty—became major government concerns.

Costa Rica's efforts to live in peace and to develop economically have also been hampered in the 1980s by the Sandinista regime in Nicaragua. Moreover, the United States has urged Costa Rica to support anti-Sandinista rebels by allowing them to use land in Costa Rica as rebel bases. Costa Rican governments have strongly refused to comply with these U.S. requests.

In 1986 Oscar Arias Sánchez won Costa Rica's presidential elections. Arias focused his presidential campaign on the need for regional peace and began working toward this goal as soon as he took office.

Guatemala Accord

In February 1987 President Arias put forth a Central American peace plan. The proposal—since referred to as the Guatemala Accord (because it was signed in that country)—aimed to ease tensions in the region. In August 1987 Arias and the chief executives of Honduras, El Salvador,

Photo by Dr. Roma Hoff

Winds in downtown San José ruffle a Costa Rican national flag. Although modified in 1964, the emblem resembles the flag of the Federation of Central America, to which Costa Rica belonged in the early nineteenth century.

Anyone is free to listen to the debates of the Legislative Assembly at the modern legislative hall.

Nicaragua, and Guatemala signed the peace plan. Its provisions included scheduled cease-fires in countries where conflict was occurring, free elections, and committees to resolve local disagreements. If carried through as written, the accord would end civil wars in Nicaragua, El Salvador, and Guatemala. In October 1987 President Arias's sponsorship of the regional initiative earned him the Nobel Prize for peace.

By late 1988, however, only Costa Rica had abided by all the provisions of the accord. Nicaragua and El Salvador enacted some of the plan's initiatives by freeing political prisoners and by meeting with their countries' rebel elements. Guatemala and Honduras have been less responsive to the accord's ideas.

Arias remains an outspoken critic of policies in Central America that he feels endanger the success of the Guatemala Accord. His efforts to bring opposing sides

together have made him a popular negotiator in several regional conflicts. But concern remains high that the Guatemala Accord—despite its balance and regional support—is some distance away from achieving its goals.

Government

Costa Rica's Constitution of 1949, proclaiming the country a free and independent democratic republic, establishes a representative form of government. Power is centralized in a federal structure with three branches—the executive, legislative, and judicial. It grants the Supreme Court the right to check the other two branches of government for any act considered unconstitutional. Other checks and balances include a presidential veto power and the power to investigate the actions of government departments, to impeach federal officials, and to limit legislative and executive terms of office.

EXECUTIVE

Executive power is vested in the president, who is assisted by two elected vice-presidents and a cabinet of the president's choice. The president is required to be a Costa Rican by birth, over 30 years of age, and a layman—that is, not a clergyman. He is chosen by direct popular election and serves for a four-year term. He cannot be reelected until after eight years have elapsed since the expiration of his term.

The duties of the chief executive include official representation of the nation, supreme command of public forces, appointment and removal of ministers, and preparation of an annual state-of-the-republic address to the legislature. The president and his cabinet ministers are known collectively as the Council of Government. The council has jurisdiction over defense and internal order, foreign affairs and international treaties, fiscal policy, nomination or removal of government officials who are not members of the civil service, and the administration of public services and agencies.

LEGISLATIVE

Lawmaking and other broad responsibilities rest with a unicameral (one-house) Legislative Assembly composed of 57 deputies, who represent numerical quotas of citizens in each of Costa Rica's provinces. The deputies are elected directly for four-year terms and cannot be reelected to successive terms of office. The assembly meets twice each year—from May 1 to July 31 and from September 1 to November 30. Special sessions may be called by the president.

A two-thirds majority of the total assembly membership may amend the constitution, and legislation may be introduced by any member or by the president. According to the constitution, the assembly has the right to enact, amend, and repeal laws; authorize declarations of war or peace; approve the national budget; levy taxes; approve or reject international agreements; suspend civil rights for periods of up to 30 days; impeach the president and censure ministers; and create courts and appoint judges.

JUDICIAL

Judicial authority is exercised by the Supreme Court of Justice and more than 100 subordinate courts of law throughout Costa Rica. There are 17 justices, or magistrates, on the Supreme Court—all of whom are elected by the Legislative Assembly. The magistrates are elected for eight-year terms and are automatically considered reelected unless voted down by a two-thirds majority of the assembly. Lower courts may appeal to the Supreme Court for final decisions.

THE CONSTITUTION

Although drawn up in 1949—at a moment of national crisis—the Costa Rican Constitution incorporates far-sighted guarantees of individual and social rights. Costa Rican citizens are afforded freedom of speech and assembly and are assured of equality before the law. No one can compel a citizen to leave the nation against his or her wishes. A citizen is granted free access to all departments of the federal administration. Any person 20 years of age or older may vote.

The constitution grants political asylum to anyone persecuted in other countries for political motives. A refugee may enter Costa Rica without fear of being forced to return to the country from which he or she fled. The constitution guarantees social security, minimum wages, overtime pay, a maximum 48-hour work week, and the right to organize trade unions.

LOCAL GOVERNMENT

For purposes of public administration, Costa Rica is divided into seven prov-

Campaign workers for the National Liberation Party offer prospective voters a ride to polling sites during the 1980 presidential elections. Large turnouts of voters have helped ensure that the Costa Rican government remains responsive to the wishes of the general public.

inces—San José, Alajuela, Cartago, Heredia, Guanacaste, Puntarenas, and Limón. The provinces, in turn, are broken down into cantons and districts.

Each province, administered by the central government, has a presidentially appointed governor to supervise law enforcement and federal employees. The provinces do not, however, have a system of self-government. Instead, self-government, or home rule, is exercised exclusively at the canton level.

The canton is responsible for administering all local services except for the police, who are provided directly by the national government. The governing body of each canton is called the *municipalidad* and is composed of a varying number of voting and nonvoting members. The voting members are referred to as *regidores* and the nonvoters as *síndicos*. They are all chosen by popular vote for four-year terms.

The municipal governments are fairly independent. They prepare their own budgets with approval from the comptroller general, the nation's top fiscal officer, and they raise their own revenue from transportation and sales taxes.

The peace of once-quiet towns like Upala near the Nicaraguan border has been interrupted by the activities of rebels seeking to overthrow Nicaragua's leftist government.

35

It is not unusual to see people on horseback in rural Costa Rica, as here on a street in the village of San Pablo de Turrubares.

3) The People

In 1988, the population of Costa Rica was estimated to be 2.9 million, making it the third most densely populated country of Central America. The population is about evenly divided between urban and rural areas.

But the advantages of population density and even distribution are to some extent offset by the fact that the population is growing at a rate of almost 3 percent per year. This means that Costa Rica has one of the highest population growth rates in the world, and its population—if the growth rate remains unchecked—will double in the next 24 years.

In order to lessen the strain of population growth on national resources, the Costa Rican government began distributing birth control information and devices in the late 1960s—steps that few other Latin American nations have taken.

Ethnic Origins

Known in Spanish as *Costarricenses,* or more familiarly as *Ticos,* Costa Ricans are proud of their racial composition, which they claim is the purest in European strains of all the peoples of Central America. Whites (descended from Spanish and other European colonists) and mestizos (people of mixed European and Indian blood) make up more than 97 percent of the total population. The exact proportion of each group, however, is not known. Unofficial statistics have placed the mestizo estimate as high as 40 percent.

The minority of greatest importance, roughly 2 percent of the population, consists of 35,000 blacks who are clustered along the Caribbean coast. Their origins can be traced back to the original slaves brought by Spanish explorers and planters, and to large numbers of black Jamaicans brought to help construct the San José–Limón railway.

Less than 1 percent of the population is pure Indian, descended from the tribes

Independent Picture Service

Farm girls with strong Indian features pass the time chatting in the sunshine.

originally encountered by Columbus. The few remaining Indians are found in northern and southern Pacific areas and along the Caribbean. They have been almost entirely assimilated into mestizo groups and retain very little of their native culture.

Newly arrived immigrants form another minor component of Costa Rica's population. They come mostly from Nicaragua and other Central American countries. Within recent years, many retired U.S. citizens have established homes in the Costa Rican highlands in order to enjoy the country's healthful climate and political stability.

Independent Picture Service

This black child is representative of Costa Rica's chief minority group. The black population dwells mainly along the Caribbean coast, but recently some blacks have moved to the highlands.

37

An archaeologist of the San José Museum catalogs pre-Columbian Indian ceramics.

Language

The official language of Costa Rica is Spanish, and Costa Ricans claim that their dialect is closer in pronunciation and vocabulary to pure Castilian Spanish than the Spanish of any other nation of the Americas except Colombia. English, the second most often heard language, is spoken by blacks of West Indian descent and is taught in all public schools. Indian dialects have almost completely disappeared.

Characteristics

By nature, Costa Ricans are easy-going, freedom-loving, friendly, and affable. Usually, they are racially tolerant and averse to social snobbery. They value marriage, and the average family has several children.

Costa Rican society is firmly rooted in the nation's Hispanic heritage, which stresses the individual but was traditionally male-dominated. Family lineage is not the lone indicator of good social standing,

Eager to learn career skills, students at the Fishing School of Puntarenas listen as Fernando Benevides shows how marine engines work.

for Costa Ricans believe in upward mobility through education and conscientiousness at work. These words appear in Costa Rica's national anthem: *Viva siempre el trabajo y la paz!* ("Long live work and peace!")

Literature

Artistic expression in all forms was slow to develop in Costa Rica for several reasons. First, preconquest Costa Rican Indians, though skilled in handicrafts, nowhere approached the greatness of the Mayan, Aztec, or Incan cultures. Also, the first Europeans in Costa Rica were homesteaders and tradespeople, not artisans. No leisure class emerged until the mid-eighteenth century. Lastly, Costa Rica was physically isolated from the intellectual capitals of colonial Latin America, the closest being Guatemala City, more than 800 miles away.

The man considered Costa Rica's national poet—Aquileo J. Echeverría—emerged in the late 1800s. His talent for writing metrical verse, combined with astute observations of his countrymen, brought him recognition throughout Central America. His best known collection of poetry is *Concherias,* which faithfully describes the land, people, and customs of his time.

The first important Costa Rican novel, not published until 1900, was *El Moto* by Joaquín García Monge, a writer of magazine articles. Another Costa Rican literary figure is Roberto Brenes Mesen—a diplomat, translator, and educator—who wrote several novels, educational tracts, and poetry. He is credited with translating Kahlil Gibran's world-famous work *The Prophet* into Spanish. Alfredo Cardona Peña resided in Mexico but composed volumes of poetry based on recollections of his Costa Rican birthplace—among them

Independent Picture Service

Josefinos, the inhabitants of San José, carry on the Spanish custom of the Sunday-afternoon *corrida de toros,* or bullfights.

Courtesy of Costa Rican Information Service

The National Theater of Costa Rica provides an ornate setting for symphony concerts, ballet performances, and dramatic productions. Built in 1897, it lends some turn-of-the-century grandeur to San José's modern business district.

Independent Picture Service

Primer Paraíso. His *Poemas Numerales* won him the coveted Central American "15th of September" literary prize. Eunice Odio of Costa Rica received the same award for her long surrealistic poem, *El Tránsito del Fuego.*

Political and social themes have become more pronounced in Costa Rica's twentieth-century literature. José María Cañas based his powerful novel *Infierno Verde* on the devastating Chaco War between Paraguay and Bolivia in the 1930s. Fabián Dobles wrote two novels, *Ese que Llaman Pueblo* and *El Sitio de las Abras,* which describe the harsh conditions of peasant life in predominantly middle-class Costa Rica. Joaquín Gutiérrez, another socially

Always a highlight of a tour of the city, San José's National Theater is patterned after the Baroque theaters of Europe. The interior of the theater has ceiling frescoes, ornate mirrors and chandeliers, carved pillars, and velvet seats.

conscious novelist, depicts the hardships endured by banana workers in the fields.

Painting, Sculpture, and Ceramics

Examples of pre-Columbian pottery from Costa Rica prove that the Indian tribes—especially the Chorotegas—did achieve some degree of artistry in ceramics and sculpture. They also crafted handsome work in gold, jade, and stone. Many figures, preserved for over 450 years and on display in San José, represent animals and spirits of Indian worship.

A Costa Rican wood engraver, Francisco Amighetti Ruíz, has become known internationally. After traveling throughout the hemisphere, he wrote and illustrated three books—*Francisco en Costa Rica, Francisco y los Caminos,* and *Francisco en Harlem.*

National folk themes, abstract forms, and surrealist traits can all be seen in the panorama of Costa Rican painting. The most typical and unique form of folk art is the hand-painted oxcart used by the peasants to haul heavy goods to and from market places. The gaily painted, intricate designs are passed from generation to generation by families. Government measures are being taken to preserve this rare art

Courtesy of David Mangurian

Although Costa Rica's decorated oxcarts are now more common in art collections than on the road, carts serving their original purpose can still sometimes be seen in rural areas.

Elaborately decorated oxcarts—to which this artist applies the finishing touches—are the form of folk art most often associated with Costa Rica.

form as automobiles and trucks take the place of oxcarts as a mode of transportation.

Crafts

Native markets and souvenir shops in Costa Rica offer an attractive selection of handmade articles. The deep brown mahogany wood of the forests is fashioned into polished bowls, trays, candlesticks, and other handcrafted objects.

Miniature replicas of Costa Rica's handpainted oxcarts are popular with tourists, who can even visit an oxcart factory near Alajuela. Other crafts include woven bas-

The Costa Rican government is encouraging the development of small businesses that make and sell native crafts.

kets and mats, embroidered cloth, figurines of mother-of-pearl and tortoise shell, and leather purses and belts.

Architecture

Violent earthquakes have crumbled into ruins many of the nation's vestiges of a colonial past. A Franciscan mission built over 300 years ago near Cartago in the village of Orosí is one of the few colonial structures to have escaped destruction. Viewing the church's carved altars and pillars, ancient religious paintings, and silver- and gold-trimmed statues and priestly vestments, one can gain an appreciation of Costa Rica's colonial artistry.

In the capital city, Spanish colonial or Renaissance architecture is still seen in some churches and public buildings. The National Theatre, built with Italian-imported marble, is a classic example of the Baroque style. Private dwellings tend to follow the lines of modern ranch-style houses of the United States and are usually constructed of wood.

Independent Picture Service

A good example of Spanish colonial architecture, El Carmen Church in Heredia shows the scars of age in its blackened walls.

Courtesy O.I.A.A. Photo

Some unusual designs can be seen in private houses in the Paseo Colón, a residential street in San José.

43

Barefoot children kneel at the altar rail of a country chapel to receive their first communion.

Religion

Although some Protestant denominations have established missions in Costa Rica, 95 percent of the people belong to the Roman Catholic Church, which is the officially recognized religion. Religious instruction is part of the public school curriculum, and the government allots about 1 percent of the national budget toward support of the Catholic Church. In spite of its privileged position, the Church has never been actively involved in the political life of the country.

Music

Costa Ricans have produced classical and modern symphonic and folk music, none of which has achieved much international prominence. Students of music were forced to study abroad until 1943, when a National Conservatory of Music was founded.

Composers worthy of mention are Julio Mata Oreamuno, who wrote *Suite Abstracta* and *Toyupán,* an operetta; Julio Fonseca Gutiérrez, known for his *Fantasía Sinfónica,* which is based on local folk songs; and César A. Nieto, who wrote the

The Church of Los Desamparados ("the Forgotten Ones") is a tourist attraction in the San José area.

Tourists from the United States take a dance lesson in San José to the accompaniment of a local musical group. The tablelike instrument in the background is a marimba, a large xylophone often played by several musicians at the same time.

ballet *La Piedra del Tóxil.* Several Costa Ricans have played classical violin and piano in concert halls abroad, and the government subsidizes a National Symphony Orchestra.

The best-preserved folk music and dances come from Guanacaste province, which still resists the inrush of urbanization. The lively *Punto Guanacaste* is the most popular of regional dances. Costa Rica's folk music is played mostly on the guitar and the marimba.

An elementary school class on a visit to the San José Museum receives a lecture on the Indian culture of Costa Rica before the arrival of the Spaniards.

Education

Costa Rica began its free educational program more than a century ago. Today the nation has one of the most progressive educational systems in the Americas. As a result, Costa Ricans have achieved a high literacy rate—95 percent.

The school system is regulated by the Ministry of Education and receives a large share of the national budget for its support. In the 1980s, the federal government contributed 23 percent of its total revenues to the public school system. Education in Costa Rica is free and compulsory for all children between the ages of 7 and 14. The school year begins in March and ends in November, enabling children and their families to enjoy the drier season of the year.

The Roman Catholic Church established the first schools in Costa Rica. These early schools were, for the most part, quite poor both financially and academically. The first university, Santo Tomás, was

At a special high school, the Colegio Técnico Profesional Agropecuario in the town of Sardinal, Marta Cubillo learns the techniques of modern agriculture and gains the background she will need to enter a university program in agronomy. Costa Rica's Ministry of Education plans to have 17 such agricultural high schools in operation soon.

established in San José in 1843; it was closed, however, by order of the Legislative Assembly 45 years later.

Interest in public education was not great until the mid-nineteenth century, when high coffee prices created enough national wealth to support a better and more extensive school system. Educational reform was led by Mauro Fernández, Minister of Education from 1885 to 1888. Under his guidance, schools were opened, textbooks written, educational laws passed, and minimum qualifications set for teachers. While in 1892 about 70 percent of the population could neither read nor write, by 1927 this figure had dropped to 25 percent.

By the 1940s, elementary and secondary schools, which until then had been located exclusively in the populous Meseta Central, had been built throughout the rest of the country. Between 1960 and the mid-1970s, the number of teachers per 10,000 pupils aged 7 to 14 increased from 223 to 251.

In 1940, the University of Costa Rica was opened in San José, with departments of law, fine arts, pharmacy, education, and agriculture. Later, schools of engineering, sciences, liberal arts, and dentistry were added, and the entire university community was transplanted to a modern university complex in the San Pedro suburb of the capital.

Vocational schools were in private hands until 1955 when two of them were converted into public institutions, laying the foundation for the federally operated vocational system of commercial, trade, and technical schools to be established later. In the early 1980s, almost 562,000 students were enrolled at all educational levels. Nursery schools accounted for 21,900; elementary schools for 348,700;

Between classes, students relax on the modern campus of the National University of Costa Rica, which has one of the highest academic reputations in Latin America.

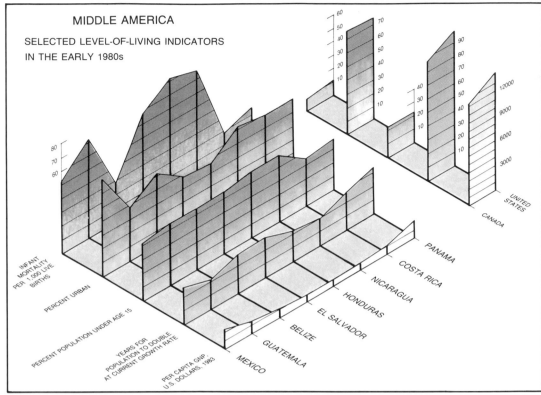

MIDDLE AMERICA

SELECTED LEVEL-OF-LIVING INDICATORS
IN THE EARLY 1980s

Artwork by Carol F. Barrett

This graph shows how each of five factors, which are suggestive of the quality and style of life, varies among the eight Middle American countries. Canada and the United States are included for comparison. Data from "1986 World Population Data Sheet" (Washington, D.C.: Population Reference Bureau, Inc., 1986).

Courtesy of United Nations

Finishing a tabletop is just part of the training to become a carpenter's apprentice.

Independent Picture Service

Women of Nicoya teach their daughters the art of dress-making.

secondary schools for 135,800; and higher education for 55,400.

Health

Improved educational opportunities are beginning to pay off in improved health conditions. Both men and women in Costa Rica now have life expectancies of more than 70 years. Infant mortality rates have dropped from 74 to 19 per thousand in the last two decades. There is one physician for approximately every 1,500 persons. Costa Rica is the only Central American republic outside of Panama in which enteritis and diarrheal diseases are not among the five leading causes of death.

Mass Media

Costa Rica's public information system is more fully developed than that of any other Central American nation. Factors contributing to this success include a free political climate, a predominantly Spanish-speaking populace, and a high literacy level. The concentration of the population in the Central Plateau facilitates distribution of news media. In addition, there is a large group of middle-class businesspersons who can support advertising.

San José, the heart of the communications industry, is home to the majority of radio and television stations, newspaper plants, and publishing houses. The most influential dailies are *La Nación, La Pren-*

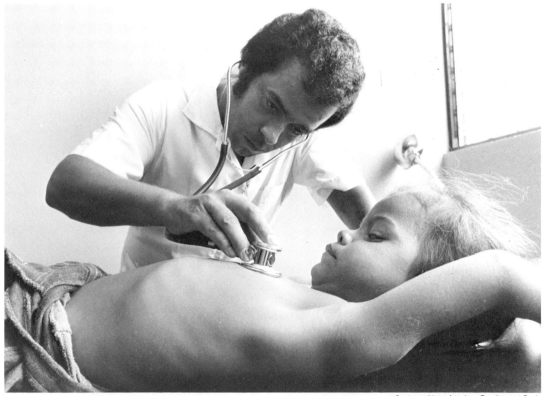

Courtesy of Inter-American Development Bank

At a rural health clinic in the Atlantic coastal town of La Perla, Dr. William Arce Campos examines three-year-old Marlyn Vega Torres, who has contracted a skin rash. Costa Rica's social security system, one of the most advanced in the hemisphere, staffs such clinics with doctors performing the year of rural service required of them by the government.

sa Libre, and La República. They are all tabloids and represent a variety of political points of view. The Tico Times is Costa Rica's English-language weekly newspaper. Radio and television stations are commercial, except for several offering religious or cultural programming. There were 190,000 radio and 250,000 television receivers operating in the 1980s.

Festivals

Costa Rica observes 11 official holidays, some religious and some patriotic. Except for Columbus Day (October 12), the nonreligious holidays are not marked by any unusual excitement. The Columbus Day celebration, however, usually lasts four days—with parades, floats, and nighttime activities—in an atmosphere resembling Carnival in other Latin nations. Other days of a nonreligious character are Labor Day (May 1), the Anniversary of the Bat-

tle of Rivas (April 11), and Independence Day (September 15).

Except for St. Joseph's Day (March 19), the Feast of St. Peter and St. Paul (June 29), and the Feast of Our Lady of the Angels (August 2), the religious holidays are Roman Catholic holy days of obligation—that is, days on which Catholics are obliged by the Church to attend services. Interestingly, Costa Ricans consider New Year's Day a more solemn holiday than Christmas. Churches are generally more crowded on January 1 than on December 25.

The Feast of Our Lady of the Angels pays homage to the patroness of Costa Rica. La Negrita, a black stone image of the Virgin Mary, is positioned atop the main altar in the Shrine of Our Lady of the Angels in Cartago. On August 2 of each year, the statuette is carried in a reverent and impressive procession from the shrine to other churches in Cartago and through the city streets. Costa Ricans are joined in this worship by pilgrims from other Central American countries and Mexico.

Sports

Like other Latin American countries, Costa Rica is devoted to soccer. Enthusiastic young boys engage in empty-lot practice sessions, dreaming of a future time when they might be accepted to play with a professional team.

Basketball, baseball, auto racing, swimming, and tennis are also popular sports. Golf and polo are played only by the wealthy; fishing, however, is enjoyed by people from all walks of life. The beaches are beautiful and are crowded between January and April.

Food

Costa Rican cooking is like that of Mexico and the other Central American countries. La Olla, "the kettle," is the most popular national dish. Served as a soup or stew, it

A trellis of lilies surrounds the tiny figure of La Negrita, Costa Rica's patron saint, as she is carried on the shoulders of paraders through the streets of Cartago on her feast day.

Costa Ricans are enthusiastic about soccer and will turn nearly any vacant lot into a playing pitch. These contestants, however, enjoy a more scenic view beside the hills of Palmar Norte in southern Costa Rica.

consists of beef, potatoes, onions, maize, beans, and tomatoes. Tamales—made of corn flour and filled with ground pork, chicken, rice, and other ingredients—are enjoyed on special occasions, as are tacos.

Other more regularly prepared foods include *tamal asado*—a pudding of sour cream, eggs, cornmeal, cheese, and sugar—and *palmito*, heart of the cabbage palm, which is served in salads and soups. A common Guanacaste dish, *gallo pinto*, is made from rice and beans that are first cooked separately and then mixed and fried together with hot chili peppers. Tortillas often supplement the typical meal of rice, beans, fruit, vegetables, eggs, coffee, fruit drinks, and a little meat.

Bananas are frequently used in puddings, pies, and cakes. Other tropical fruits, such as mangoes, papayas, and *granadillas* (passion fruit), are used in a variety of desserts and salads.

Baskets of native herbs and flowers hang from the porch roof of a country house.

While her brother Berny uses a smoker to tranquilize the bees, Roxana Cordero Quiroz of Santa María de Dota checks the hives from which she will harvest honey. Her business grew out of her membership in the Costa Rican equivalent of a 4-H Club. These clubs involve young people in community activities and help them learn practical skills.

4) The Economy

Costa Rica's economy operates mainly in accordance with the principles of free, private enterprise. The mainstay of the economy is agriculture, which generates 65 percent of Costa Rica's export earnings and employs 35 percent of its work force.

As might be expected of a small nation, Costa Rica is greatly affected by economic forces beyond its control. Ups and downs of world prices for some of its most important commodity exports—coffee, bananas, and sugar—have historically caused a boom-and-bust cycle that the country's

authorities have not always been able to moderate.

Agriculture

The Costa Rican government has played an important role in developing agriculture. Government-sponsored research investigates ways to increase the productivity of the land and cattle-raising operations. Government-backed loans help farmers to settle new lands, develop new crops for which there is export demand, in-

A worker uses a machete to strip the bark from a young tree.

troduce irrigation, and boost per-acre harvests of such traditional crops as coffee, cacao, rice, beans, and potatoes. Extension agents bring technical assistance to farmers where they need it—on their farms.

Such efforts have yielded good results. The nation now largely feeds itself (though it still must import some wheat), and it has increasing surpluses to export. For more than a decade, agricultural production has increased faster than the nation's population.

COFFEE

Coffee was cultivated in Costa Rica for the first time in 1779 and by the 1820s had already become the nation's chief export crop. Costa Rica's annual yield, about 120,000 tons, is the third largest in Central America. The high-grade beans, known for their robust flavor, are grown mostly on the Central Plateau, in the San José Basin and the Turrialba Valley.

The trend of recent years has been the creation of larger and larger coffee plantations, known as *fincas,* through mergers. Five percent of these fincas now produce half of the yearly crop. Owners of these plantations constitute a powerful economic interest group. They have their own organizations and social clubs and publish magazines to stimulate awareness of the latest developments in the coffee-growing field.

Despite the importance of the large land-

When ripe, coffee beans must be picked by hand, though other phases of coffee production have been mechanized.

Coffee berries – or "cherries," as they are usually called – are turned repeatedly by plantation hands for 10 to 14 days to provide even drying by the sun. Later the beans are shelled, sorted, and bagged for shipment.

holders, there is still room for the small producer. The other half of Costa Rica's coffee is produced on fincas of less than 25 acres. The bulk of the coffee harvest is sold to coffee-processing companies in the United States and West Germany.

BANANAS

In Costa Rica, bananas have been second to coffee as an export crop since the early 1900s. Diseases that ravaged the banana plants in the 1930s forced producers to transfer major plantations from the Caribbean lowlands to the Pacific coastal area, where irrigation is necessary. In recent years, however, banana planters have successfully developed disease-resistant varieties, and the Caribbean coast once again supports banana cultivation. Bananas now can compete with coffee for first place – in monetary terms – among Costa Rica's exports. Unlike coffee, which is grown almost entirely by Costa Ricans,

bananas are grown mainly by foreign-owned companies—the largest of which is United Brands.

SUGAR

Sugar emerged as an important export crop only recently, in the late 1950s. At that time, the United States stopped buying sugar from Cuba—formerly its main supplier—in reaction to the Communist takeover there. Since then, half of Costa Rica's total production has been exported to the United States. In the early 1980s, Costa Rican sugar exports were earning about $2.5 million annually. Most of the crop is produced on small farms that are widely scattered throughout the nation, with concentration in the provinces of Alajuela, Cartago, and San José.

The morning egg hunt has been a success at one of the chicken houses at the Costa Rican Incubating Company. These eggs, along with chickens for frying, will be shipped to the grocery stores of San José, while baby chicks raised here will be sent to other poultry raisers throughout the country.

Ripe cacao pods (used in making chocolate) are ready to be harvested at La Lola Farm, a hub of cacao production. In the eighteenth century, when currency was scarce, cacao pods were used as legal tender. The pods grow directly from the trunk and are easily dislodged by the wind.

CACAO

Cacao, the source of cocoa and chocolate, was the first cash crop ever grown in Costa Rica. The Nahua Indians brought cacao seed with them when they emigrated from Mexico in the fourteenth century. Since the 1600s, cacao—though a risky crop to raise because the fruit must grow in shade and be free from high winds—has been a source of substantial revenue. Costa Rica produces more than $1 million worth of cacao annually, mostly in the Puerto Limón area.

After these cacao beans have been inspected and sorted, the best will be used in making chocolate candy at a plant near the Caribbean coast. The Caribbean lowlands have supported cacao cultivation since pre-Columbian times.

On this experimental plot, a high-yield, disease-resistant bean is being developed.

OTHER CROPS

Maize, rice, beans, tobacco, potatoes, other vegetables, and fruits make up the remainder of Costa Rica's principal farm crops. These are grown almost exclusively for domestic consumption. Fishing and forest products may one day become valuable revenue-earners for the small nation, but as yet they are underdeveloped. Quantities of rosewood, cedar, mahogany, and other cabinet woods are to be found in the forests.

LIVESTOCK

The breeding of livestock for meat and dairy products has become an important agricultural activity in recent years. Guanacaste Province is the main cattle-producing region, followed in importance by the San Carlos district in Alajuela Province. From these areas, live animals and frozen beef are exported to other areas of Central America, the Caribbean islands

A farmer grazes his milk cows on slopes enriched by old lava flows from the nearby Irazú Volcano.

Guernsey and holstein cows, carefully bred to produce a maximum amount of milk, head to pasture along with steers in Guanacaste province. In recent years, raising beef and dairy cattle has become a very important business in Costa Rica.

(especially Puerto Rico), and the United States.

A modern dairy industry has been developed on the Central Plateau. Jersey, guernsey, and holstein cows are bred, and milk production is high. Experts believe that dairy output can be increased by the use of improved cattle feeds.

Research in the field of agriculture is carried out by the School of Agriculture at the University of Costa Rica in San José and at the Inter-American Institute of Agricultural Sciences in Turrialba—formerly an agency of the Organization of American States.

Cosme Mata Fonseca transfers seedlings of fast-growing Australian cedar to bottomless metal pots. A research program in Turrialba has shown that when the roots of seedlings in bottomless pots reach the air, they stop growing and spread out into thick clusters that make the young trees easier to plant. Because Turrialba, in east central Costa Rica, has a climate typical of Latin American farming areas, it has long been a center of agricultural research.

Farm workers weigh a watermelon harvested on a cooperative farm on the Nicoya Peninsula.

The citizens of Puerto Jiménez build a road using government-owned equipment.

Government Sector

The government is Costa Rica's second largest employer after agriculture, providing jobs for approximately 25 percent of the labor force. Many of these workers have jobs at one of about 130 so-called autonomous institutions—agencies that, while government-funded, operate independently of either executive or legislative control. The justification for this modification of the free enterprise system is found in the 1949 constitution, which makes the state responsible for the social and economic well-being of the people, as well as the educational and cultural development of society.

Among the better known of such institutions are the Central Bank of Costa Rica, Costa Rican Railroads, Costa Rican Airlines, the University of Costa Rica, and the Costa Rican Social Security Fund. Other such agencies promote tourism, vocational education, campaigns against alcoholism, scientific and technological research, housing and urban development, chemical distilling, agrarian reform, and community development. Major autonomous institutions include the Costa Rican Institute of Electricity, which administers the nation's power grid, and the Costa Rican Development Corporation, which administers large sums of money in promoting economic development.

Other major employers within the government sector are the bureaucracies that administer the nation at the provincial level.

Industry

Manufacturing is growing swiftly in Costa Rica and presently employs almost one-fourth of the work force. As might be expected in a nation historically so dependent on farming, food processing remains the largest single industry. Among the main foods and beverages produced are tinned fruits, vegetables, and meats; edible oils; instant coffee; and beer and alcohol. The Costa Rican chemical industry turns out plastics, paints, fertilizer, insecticides, soaps, cosmetics, nylon hosiery, and pharmaceutical products. Textiles, clothing, shoes, other leather items, tires, plywood, and furniture are also manufactured in local plants. The building trades use locally produced cement and construction materials.

The growth of industry was stimulated by the 1959 Industrial Development Law, which provides attractive incentives for manufacturers, including profitable government contracts.

The Common Market

Costa Rica's industrial growth was also given a substantial boost by the formation of the Central American Common Market (CACM) in 1963. The CACM, comprising Guatemala, Honduras, Nicaragua, El Salvador, and Costa Rica, helped to stimulate industrial expansion by opening up the market potential of all five countries to new industries located in the area.

The arrangement functioned very well and led to the quintupling of trade among its five member nations—up until the outbreak of a war between two members, El Salvador and Honduras, in 1969. The CACM has yet to recover fully from the hostilities and antagonisms caused by that conflict. Unfortunately, Costa Rica contributed to the ailing health of the common market by buying much more from its Central American partners than it sold to them, in part because of Costa Rica's consumerism.

Moreover, to make it easier for Costa Rica to liquidate its debts, the nation's Central Bank adopted inequitable exchange rates for CACM transactions. It sold its goods at a high rate of exchange, 8.57 colones (the national currency) to the U.S. dollar, but bought low from Costa Rica's partners, at a rate of only 6.65 colones to the dollar.

Reacting against this unfair practice, other common market nations broke off their trade with Costa Rica in September 1972, and President Figueres retaliated by threatening to withdraw permanently. Since then, a series of high-level meetings in San José have ironed out some of the

Courtesy of Inter-American Development Bank

Costa Rica is well endowed with tropical hardwoods. The wood processed at a mill in Bijagua will go into the making of durable, richly grained furniture.

59

difficulties. The Costa Ricans have devalued their own currency, and CACM trade has been resumed. Nonetheless, the regional group has been substantially weakened.

Transportation

Planes, trains, and highways connect Costa Rica's major cities and ports. Highways were first built on the self-contained Central Plateau, and, until recent years, most of the nation's highlanders had never visited the lowland areas of the nation. In the last several decades, the government has devoted a great deal of money to the construction of highways. Lacsa, the nation's main airline, flies both international and internal routes, and eight other companies are licensed as domestic carriers.

Costa Rica has about 775 miles of railroads, all of 42-inch gauge. About half are owned by United Brands. The Northern Railway connects San José with Limón,

Passenger and freight trains connect Puerto Limón on the Atlantic coast with San José in the highlands. The first tracks were laid in the 1880s by Minor Keith, a U.S. construction expert.

The Colorado Bridge, with its distinctive "upside-down" central span, is on the road from San José to Puntarenas.

the nation's principal Caribbean seaport. The Ferrocarril Eléctrico al Pacífico connecting San José with Puntarenas is government-owned. The Costa Rican portion of the Pan-American Highway is about 300 miles in length. In addition, there are about 12,000 miles of roads, mostly unsurfaced.

The old and the new in transportation—cargo is transferred from oxcart to aircraft at San Isidro, a provincial town.

61

Workmen build a tunnel for a hydro-electric project.

The La Garita hydroelectric power plant, a 30,000-kilowatt operation, was inaugurated in 1958. It harnesses the energy of three rivers: the Tizate, Alajuela, and Río Grande de Tárcoles.

Giant diesel motors are at work inside the La Garita plant.

Electric Power

Costa Rica derives nearly all of its electric power from hydroelectric sources. The three largest plants are all located on the Central Plateau, but they feed into an extensive national grid. This efficient distribution network is one reason Costa Rica has the second highest per capita consumption of energy in Central America. Bagasse, the residue from squeezed sugarcane, is being used successfully for fuel by industry, but other fuels must be imported to take care of domestic needs.

Foreign Trade, Aid, and Investment

As Costa Rica entered the mid-1980s, the value of its exports declined, and stringent efforts were being made to reduce imports as well. The country's principal imports are machinery (including transport equipment), manufactured goods, chemicals, fuel and mineral oils, and foodstuffs, especially grain. Its principal exports in terms of earnings are coffee, bananas, chemicals, beef, and sugar. Most of Costa Rica's trade is with the United States, Western Europe, Japan, and other Central American republics.

In the early 1980s the government was facing an external public debt that approached $5 billion, leading to inflation rates of more than 20 percent annually. As a result of the country's fiscal problems, financial aid from the International Monetary Fund (IMF) and the United States Agency for International Development was cut off in late 1983. Rescheduling agreements with U.S. creditor banks were made conditional upon new arrangements with the IMF. Disbursements, however, were subsequently held up as objections to the IMF terms in the Costa Rican Legislative Assembly delayed the signing of a letter of intent. Costa Rica then had to seek $50 million in emergency funds from Mexico to prevent defaulting on its debt payments.

Courtesy of Inter-American Development Bank

A successful fishing cooperative at Puntarenas offers training for young apprentices who wish to learn the trade.

The Future

The government of Costa Rica knows the country must work hard and receive financial help from abroad if it is to progress economically and socially. Of primary importance is a reversal of the decline in the nation's balance of payments.

The reduction of imports and expansion of exports continues to dominate the government's plans. Traditional exports, like bananas and coffee, must be increased and emphasis given to selling more manufactured items in world markets. Research must continue into new ways to realize the potential of the nation's land, forest, and fishing resources.

Politically, Costa Rica is also addressing its national concerns. Although a democratic form of government has been working successfully for 40 years, the nation still lies in a region of tension. Through the Guatemala Accord, efforts to confront and resolve those conflicts have been underway since 1987. Whether or not Costa Rica will be able to engineer lasting peace in the region remains to be seen. But the small, peaceful nation has unquestionably taken an important step in achieving that goal.

Index